Ross and Cron Coast to Coast

Text by Gi

Introduction

In the far north of Scotland, where summer daylight lingers on the hilltops till late in the evening, there lies a region with its own exclusive magic – Ross and Cromarty.

Dividing by geography naturally into two parts, Easter and Wester Ross lie on either side of the austere ridges of the backbone of Scotland. The eastern side has rolling farmlands, forests, a coastline thronged with birdlife – but always the sense of looming hills on the western horizon. Wester Ross itself offers a dramatic experience of rock architecture surpassed in few, if any, other parts of Scotland. Both should be visited – east–west roads are good and the new A9 speeds the visitor over the spectacular Kessock Bridge beyond Inverness and into the far north.

A little exploring in Easter Ross and the visitor will soon appreciate where *exactly* this land lies in relation to the rest of Scotland. From the high points of the Black Isle peninsula, for example, the Moray coast is clearly visible southwards, backed by the outliers of the Grampians as part of this southern panorama; while on the other hand, the hills of Strathconon, the Fannichs above Achnasheen and Ben Wyvis are clearly identifiable, marking where the lowland settlements have given way to the mountain barrier.

Of Wester Ross, scenic adjectives are hardly adequate to describe the great terraces of Liathach looming in the

Below: *Liathach and Loch Clair.*
Ci-dessous: *Liathach et le loch Clair.*
Unten: *Liathach und Loch Clair.*

Torridons, or the ghostly pinnacles of Stac Pollaidh as they erode into brittle screes. Some of the very best scenery lies far from the public road, in true wilderness country – but a hint of it can be gained in tantalising glimpses northwards from Loch Maree-side, or on the emotively-named Destitution Road between Dundonnell and Ullapool. Untamed, ancient landscapes are also on view from the fast route from Garve to Ullapool: Ben Dearg and its satellites, with their rare alpine plants and trackless interior – the very heart of the far north-west.

The coastlines themselves have their own special appeal. Eastwards, the Cromarty and Beauly Firths bite deeply into the lowlands. The former has long associations as a deep-water naval anchorage. Now the Sutors of Cromarty – as the guarding headlands are named – have witnessed in the 1970s in particular, the construction and float-out of deep-water platforms for the oil industry. But such is the scale of the landscape that it absorbs such industrial intrusions and the visitor is left with impressions only of endless beaches and sandflats with oystercatchers flickering and piping, or spectacular seascapes on the east shore near Cromarty where once the self-taught Hugh Miller chipped apart fossil fish and unlocked the secrets of the old red sandstones.

Although sandy beaches are to be found in the west, notably at Gairloch, sea coast and mountain top are close enough together to ensure dramatic coastal encounters. Hillwalkers in this part of Scotland well appreciate precisely what height above *sea-level* really means – with the coast so prominently seen from many tops. This proximity of sea and high ground also creates a complex and ever-changing weather pattern that can, for example, leave Inverewe Gardens sunlit and glowing, while clouds lour over the peaks a few miles inland.

Inevitably, it is the landscapes that leave the lasting impressions – the mottled marbling of the rocks on the shore at Eathie on the Black Isle; the panoramic, 'arm's length' view of hill masses from Tarbat Ness lighthouse far out in the east; the last lowland fields glimpsed from Contin en route for the west; the sheltered crescent of Shieldaig on its curved bay; ancient relic pines rooted on even older rock-faces on Loch Maree – these will be your souvenirs of Ross and Cromarty.

Aux confins Nord de l'Ecosse, là où la lumière d'été illumine les collines tard dans la soirée, s'étend une région au charme mystérieux: Ross et Cromarty.

Ross se divise en deux parties: Est et Ouest (Easter et Wester) situées de part et d'autre d'austères escarpements rocheux. Aux prairies ondulées et forêts à l'Est répondent les spectaculaires formations rocheuses à l'Ouest.

Vue des hauteurs de la péninsule de Black Isle dans Easter Ross, la côte de Moray se découpe clairement vers le Sud avec au fond les monts Grampians, tandis que par ailleurs les collines de Strathconon, les Fannichs au-dessus d'Achnasheen et Ben Wyvis se distinguent nettement.

A l'Ouest les adjectifs font défaut pour qualifier les vastes terrasses de Liathach dans les Torridons ou les pointes mystérieuses de Stac Pollaidh. Les plus beaux paysages sont généralement inaccessibles par la route mais on peut s'en faire une idée au Nord du loch Maree-side, de la route entre Dundonnell et Ullapool (« Destitution Road »). De la voie rapide entre Garve et Ullapool on bénéficie aussi de beaux panoramas sur Ben Dearg, cœur même de ce sauvage Nord-Ouest.

Les estuaires (firths) de Cromarty et Beauly s'en foncent profondément dans les terres et malgré la construction de plates-formes de forage pour le pétrole, la beauté du paysage triomphe toujours, avec ses longues plages où les oiseaux de mer abondent.

A l'Ouest la côte présente des escarpements rocheux qui tombent à pic dans la mer, faisant la joie des randonneurs. Cette topographie est responsable d'un micro-climat singulier: le littoral peut-être ensoleillé tandis que les sommets, à quelques kilomètres de là sont couverts de nuages.

Les paysages de Ross et Cromarty laisseront au visiteur des souvenirs inoubliables, que ce soient les rochers d'Eathie, le panorama du sommet du phare de Tarbat Ness ou les sapins du loch Maree.

Im hohen Norden Schottlands, wo das Tageslicht noch am späten Abend auf den Berggipfeln verweilt, liegt eine Landschaft mit ihrem eigenen Zauber – Ross und Cromarty.

Geographisch auf natürliche Weise in zwei Teile geteilt liegen Easter und Wester Ross je auf einer Seite der kahlen Berggrate Schottlands. Die Ostseite schmückt sanft welliges Ackerland, Wälder und eine Küste mit den verschiedensten Vogelarten, die Landschaft von Wester Ross findet in ihrer dramatischen Szenerie nicht ihresgleichen in anderen Teilen Schottlands. Beide Teile sollten besucht werden. Die Straßen sind gut und die neue A9-Straße bringt den Besucher schnell über Inverness bis in den hohen Norden.

Für Wester Ross fehlen Worte, die die Riesenterrassen von Liathach hinreichend beschreiben könnten, oder die geisterhaften Gipfel von Stac Pollaidh. Die schönste Szenerie liegt abseits der Straßen in wahrer wilder, unberührter Landschaft mit seltenem, alpinen Pflanzenwuchs und wo alle Wege enden.

Left: *Stac Pollaidh from Loch Lurgainn.*
A gauche: *le mont Stac Pollaidh.*
Links: *Stac Pollaidh von Loch Lurgainn gesehen.*

Die Küste hat ihren eigenen Reiz. Im Osten haben die Cromarty und Beauly Fjörde tiefe Einkerbungen in das Tiefland geschnitten. Beauly Firth war schon immer Ankerplatz für Marineschiffe. Die Sutors of Cromarty – wie die Landzunge heißt – ist in den siebziger Jahren für die Ölförderung erschlossen worden. Doch ist die Landschaft so endlos und weit, daß sie solch industrielle Übergriffe durchaus verkraftet.

Im Westen, hauptsächlich bei Gairloch, drängen sich Küste und Berge eng zusammen und bewirken so eine überaus dramatische Küstenlandschaft. Die Nähe von See und hohen Bergen schafft außerdem ein ständig wechselndes Wetter.

Es ist die Landschaft, die letztlich den bleibenden Eindruck hinterläßt – die marmorierten Felsen an den Ufern bei Eathie auf der Schwarzen Insel – die panoramaartige, „entrückte" Ansicht der Bergmassen vom Tarbat Ness Leuchtturm nach Osten – die letzten Tieflandfelder von Contin auf dem Weg nach Westen – der geschützte, sichelförmige Bogen des Shieldaig – uralte, knorrige Kiefern, die ihre Wurzeln in noch älteres Gestein krallen am Loch Maree – all dies wird Ihre Erinnerung an Ross und Cromarty sein.

Hillwalking

With soaring ridges seemingly on every horizon, Ross and Cromarty inevitably attracts attention from hill-walking enthusiasts. If the mountains themselves are spectacular, they also fall into two main categories – extremely popular or extremely remote. Into the first of these categories must fall the Torridons. The grey slopes of Beinn Eighe cascade their quartzite blocks down from their sandstone foundations almost to the road through the glen. The summit ridge is craggy and not for the faint-hearted. Great caution is also necessary on its westerly neighbour Liathach with its own amazing pinnacles offering the choice between an airy scramble or a more cautious traverse. Yet further beyond lies Beinn Alligin with its distinct profile. The so-called 'horns' of Alligin also offer a challenge to the ordinary southern fell-walker.

Back in Easter Ross, the broad whaleback of Ben Wyvis offers a spectacular panorama and a much less dizzying foothold, though its moorland bulk holds snow till late in the season. It dominates the eastern skylines and is a long pull upward from the main road towards Garve.

The dedicated collector of 'Munros' – mountains in Scotland over 3,000 feet (or a less romantic 914 metres) in height – will have a wide choice. However, some of the very finest hills do not achieve this over-emphasised verticality. Stac Pollaidh in the Inverpolly National Nature Reserve is barely over 2,000 feet (609 metres) but has more interest than many mountains nearly twice its height. Its shattered blocks and eroding claws and buttresses are a weird spectacle from all angles, inviting scrambling and exploration. Cul Mor, one of its near neighbours, is a fine viewpoint for the constellations of tiny lochans that catch the summer sun and throng this part of Wester Ross near its northern borders.

South of Dundonnell, with a strong sense of remoteness, is An Teallach, a fanged ridge glimpsed over rolling moorland from the Ullapool–Dundonnell road. It offers spectacular airy ridges reached after a respectable trek – and is another peak not for the timid. But amid all this drama there are many fine hills often overlooked. Upper Strathconon offers a mini-ridge walk on Sgurr a' Mhuilinn, which is the peak, more easily climbed than pronounced, seen to best advantage from the bridge over the River Meig near the hotel. From the top, a great harmony of hills ring the skyline, from the Glen Cannich peaks in the south, the familiar Torridons north-westwards, round the northern rim to Wyvis again – with the Sutors of Cromarty on the east coast as a reminder of the lowlands.

And for the casual walkers who want reward without too much effort, there are the Applecross Hills, the great buttresses and corries of Beinn Bhan – into which the walker can look, if after spiralling up to over 2,000 feet by car on the Bealach nam Ba, this high road is the walk's starting point.

For the fit and experienced, there are expeditions deep into trackless territory, with overnight bivouacking a necessity – as, in essence, the wildest country anywhere in the British Isles lies in Wester Ross. Local advice should be sought particularly in late summer when the stalking season is under way. Not all walkers will reach the remote ridges and, fortunately, casual walkers will find plenty of choice – and an inspiration in the spectacular skylines.

Top left: *Cul Mor, Cul Beag and Stac Pollaidh seen from the coast;* **bottom left:** *the most westerly of the Torridon mountains, Beinn Alligin overlooks Loch Torridon;* **below:** *Suilven offers a challenge to the hillwalker, with its long summit ridge several miles from public roads.*

A gauche, en haut: *les monts Cul Mor, Cul Beag et Stac Pollaidh vus du littoral;* **à gauche en bas:** *Beinn Alligin, surplombant le loch Torridon, est le plus occidental des monts Torridon;* **ci-dessous:** *le mont Suilven, avec sa longue crête éloignée des routes, est un défi aux amateurs d'escalade.*

Oben links: *Cul Mor, Cul Beag und Stac Pollaidh von der Küste gesehen;* **unten links:** *der westlichste der Torridon Berge, Beinn Alligin überschaut Loch Torridon;* **unten:** *dem Bergwanderer bietet Suilven mit seinem langen, schmalen Grat eine Herausforderung. Er liegt einige Kilometer von den Straßen entfernt.*

Easter Ross and the Black Isle

Climatic conditions are among the many contrasts east and west, noticeable in the area around Tarbat Ness lighthouse, for example. It boasts one of the lowest rainfall figures in Scotland. This adds to the attractiveness of sheltered Portmahomack nearby with its safe sandy beach and small harbour. Just over the rolling cultivated headland lies tiny Rockfield on the sea edge, offering a pleasant walk along the rocky coast to the stark ruins of Z-plan Ballone Castle.

Tain, overlooking the long, open flats and dunes of the Morich More, is a Royal Burgh of some antiquity, with a fine museum, varied architecture and an association as a place of pilgrimage for Scottish kings of former times.

Further to the south-west is Evanton. Above the village on Cnoc Fyrish is a strange hilltop monument dating from 1782. From a distance it appears as a

Left: *Falls of Rogie, near Contin;* **below:** *Tarbat Ness Lighthouse.*
A gauche: *les chutes de Rogie;* **ci-dessous:** *le phare de Tarbat Ness.*
Links: *Wasserfälle von Rogie bei Contin;* **unten:** *Tarbat Ness Leuchtturm.*

gathering of strange totem-pole-like structures but is, in fact, a replica of the Indian gateway at Seringapatam. General Sir Hector Munro distinguished himself in the Indian Campaign and on his return to his native land decided to build the gateway as a monument and to provide local work.

But Evanton's most unusual attraction lies behind the town. The remarkable Black Rock Gorge is a geological freak with few parallels anywhere else in the country. (Visitors should park on the public road and walk to this unsignposted spot.) The length and depth of the dark chasm are spectacular enough, but its oddest feature is its extreme narrowness – the dark green, slippery, mossy walls only a few feet apart in places with the glint of waters nearly 200 feet below barely visible. Not a place for the vertigo sufferer – and it has the reputation of being haunted!

More easily photographed and altogether cheerier are the Falls of Rogie, beyond Contin. This pleasant spot has a selection of nature trails, a suspension bridge of disconcerting elasticity, and a fine sylvan atmosphere of birch and pine.

The commercial centre for the area is Dingwall, which, like Tain, is a settlement of great antiquity. This is echoed in the origins of its name, dating from its eleventh-century Norse settlement – 'thing-vollr' – 'the place of justice'. Little remains now of its castle, though an ancient hill fort, its outline barely detected in the grass on Knockfarrel Hill nearby, is also a reminder of early colonisers of the once swampy valley running back towards Strathpeffer. Nowadays, Dingwall bustles with through-traffic and a wide range of shops set in its varied styles of domestic architecture.

Its neighbour Strathpeffer, has, by contrast, an air of faded Victorian gentility. If Dingwall has a tradition as a commercial centre for the area, then Strathpeffer was its resort; not only a gateway westwards, but in its Victorian heyday, a famous spa centre. The sulphurous springs, authorities assure the visitor, are among the best in Britain and – though the splendid hotels no longer throng with consumptive and arthritic Victorians taking the cure – today's tourists can still sample the

Below: *the Kessock Bridge bypasses Inverness.*
Ci-dessous: *le pont de Kessock.*
Unten: *die Kessock Brücke umgeht Inverness.*

waters. The restoration of the old railway station, on the now-closed terminus of the Strathpeffer branch, is an appropriate monument to its former bustling times.

In the vicinity is the Eagle Stone, an ancient Celtic carved slab, now serving to commemorate the turning of the forces of Donald of the Isles by the local Munro clan, in their attempt to seize Dingwall Castle in 1411.

Visitors should also take time to visit the Black Isle. Of various explanations given for the origin of its name, the most favoured seems to be that it refers to the colour and fertile nature of its soil. Certainly, it is a well-tilled area, where it is not covered in dark forests – which provide another explanation for the name in themselves. Since the building of the Kessock Bridge, visitors eager for fine coastal scenery can find themselves

in the peninsula's rolling farmlands, having bypassed Inverness altogether. Noting the Nature Reserve at Munlochy Bay and the houses at Avoch placed gable-end to the sea, the traveller soon reaches Fortrose and Rosemarkie. The former has an imposing ruined cathedral dating from the fourteenth and fifteenth centuries, as well as a peaceful square of buildings scattered around it, while the latter has an interesting museum at Groam House. As the road pulls out of Rosemarkie, twisting inland to gain height, the visitor should note the entrance to the Fairy Glen, with stream and tall mixed woodland threaded by a sheltered path through the valley.

Below: *Fortrose Cathedral.*
Ci-dessous: *la cathédrale de Fortrose.*
Unten: *Fortrose Kathedrale.*

Strathconon

Portrait of a Highland Glen

Although Easter and Wester Ross appear as two separate personalities on either side of the comparative emptiness of the interior, there is a linking element. Sometimes overlooked, as it is not a through route from coast to coast, except for sturdy walkers, the long glen of Strathconon starts in the fertile, drier farmlands of the east before twisting deep into the western hill masses. On its way it shows aspects of Highland and Lowland, harmonising the very finest features of each.

The first aspect of life in the glen is soon noticeable to the visitor who has decided to leave the main road at Marybank and head for the inviting hills. The hydro-electric dam at Torrachilty is the lowest dam in the Strathconon catchment area, a network of mainly unseen pipework and reservoirs, the scale of which is in keeping with the scenery. Beyond Torrachilty, to north and west are engineering works, mostly hidden after their construction in the 1950s, and in any case mellowed in the landscape.

Another mellowing or softening feature in the landscape in the very centre of Scotland is the Forestry Commission's planting schemes, with the dark green pines interlaced with the russet of the winter-bare larches. Mixed forests march up the slopes as the visitor ascends the valley. These trees echo the ancient forests that they replaced, which themselves had equally old-established tracks across the country. In Strathconon, some of these old tracks have been opened up in a series of forest walks. Red squirrels and pine martens are only two of the rewards for the visitor who leaves the road.

But the most conspicuous mammal in the glen is the red deer. In the upper parts, beyond the East Lodge Hotel, deer commonly descend to the river flats. In autumn, the crags echo to the roaring stags. With stalking an important local industry, some supplementary winter food is provided by local landowners and as a result the high slopes of the upper glen support a substantial deer population. Even so, visitors may still have to look carefully, as the wintery russet shades of bracken and dark heather provide good camouflage at a distance.

It is from the high corries, into which in summer the deer retreat, that the walker too, can best appreciate the various activities in the glen below. From the slopes of Sgurr a' Mhuilinn (the shapely hill that dominates the view from the bridge below the glen's only hotel) can be

seen the little community of Strathconon itself – church, village hall, farms and a scattering of cottages. Eastwards, hazily hanging above the tiny grey wall of the dam, the Sutors of Cromarty are on the skyline, beyond the distant symmetry of the new road-bridge over the Firth itself, as a reminder of lowland industry and speedy communications. In contrast, back at lower levels at the head of the glen, the public road ends, as does scenic Loch Beannacharain, the seldom disturbed haunt of goosander, pochard, and other duck. Through the pass beyond lies Achnasheen, or yet further west, Achnashellach, 'the field of the willows', both communities served by through routes and rail connections which do not disturb Strathconon.

The visitor should wait a little, in the tranquillity of silent slopes and lapping water, for a glimpse of a golden eagle is a possibility, as testimony to an undisturbed landscape. Such a view would make an interesting comparison in size with the telegraph-pole-perching buzzards, seen commonly in the glen (and often called 'tourists' eagles' by the more humorous of the locals).

From its outfall in the Lowlands to its peaceful upper reaches, this typical glen has revealed many aspects of Highland life; industries that blend with landscape, such as hydro-electric power and forestry; sporting activities such as deer-stalking or fishing; landscape features as a reminder of an ice-age that finally melted away only a few thousand years ago – the glen itself at several points showing the classic U-shape of a glacial valley. With its steep craggy slopes, plunging waters and conspicuous wildlife, it is the very essence, in little more than a score of miles, of Ross and Cromarty.

Below: *goosander;* **bottom:** *pine marten;* **far left:** *Strathconon, in the heart of Ross and Cromarty.*

Ci-dessous: *harle;* **en bas:** *martre;* **page de gauche:** *le mont Strathconon, situé au cœur de la région de Ross et Cromarty.*

Unten: *Gänsesäger;* **darunter:** *Baummarder;* **ganz links:** *Strathconon liegt im Herzen von Ross und Cromarty.*

Before reaching Cromarty, to the north, the Eathie Burn and its outflow on the shore demands attention. It certainly did from the nineteenth-century stonemason, self-taught geologist and writer, Hugh Miller, Cromarty's most famous son. In the deep and tangled channel of the burn itself, he discovered whole ranges of fossil fish in the local sandstones, working in complete intellectual isolation, till the significance of his systematic researches drew the attention of scientists outside.

Above: *Hugh Miller's Cottage.*
Ci-dessus: *la maison de Hugh Miller.*
Oben: *Hugh Millers Cottage.*

Visitors (after being sensible about parking) can make their way down to the shore at the old fishing station at Eathie. The peaceful coastline, with its steep grassy slopes from the cultivated fields above, provides ample opportunities to hunt in rock-pools, admire the fantastic shapes of water-worn rocks and muse upon the patience and perseverance of Hugh Miller himself. (The direct route from road to shore via the burn itself is not advised – and is best left alone by the ordinary pedestrian.)

The cottage that was Miller's birthplace at Cromarty in 1802, is now in the care of the National Trust for Scotland. It contains relics from his days as a stonemason, as well as displays illustrating his achievements in letters and geology. The town itself sits squarely on a promontory with the two great headlands, the Sutors of Cromarty, guarding the Firth itself to the east. There are some fine seventeenth- and eighteenth-century buildings, particularly the parish church with its woodwork which includes box pews, a poor's loft and a laird's loft.

Below: *the Sutors of Cromarty guard the narrow entrance to the deep-water anchorage of the Cromarty Firth – the north Sutor is shown here;* **overleaf:** *Loch Achilty, Easter Ross.*
Ci-dessous: *les monts Sutor de Cromarty dominent l'entrée étroite de l'estuaire de Cromarty – on voit ici le mont septentrional;* **page suivante:** *le loch Achilty dans l'Easter Ross.*
Unten: *Die Sutors von Cromarty überschauen den engen Eingang zum Tiefwasserankerplatz der Cromerty Fjörde – hier ist der Nord Sutor gezeigt;* **umseitig:** *Loch Achilty, Easter Ross.*

Wester Ross

Wester Ross, particularly the northern part, is undoubtedly for the connoisseur of the wildest and grandest scenery. None of the softness and lush sylvan shades of Argyll or Perthshire is here. The landscape makes an uncompromising statement in its great ribs of bare rock and fantastic buttressed mountains. Roads tend to the coast wherever possible, though the main route from Ullapool up and through Coigach towards Assynt is now fast and much improved.

Ullapool, the largest town in these parts, with a population of over 1,000, was founded by the Fisheries Association as a planned settlement in 1788. With its regular grid of streets, it is still an important fishing port and, in certain seasons, Loch Broom fills with fishing vessels of many nations including the Eastern Bloc, contributing a cosmopolitan flavour to this northern community. Loch Broom points far inland, but yet further eastwards in the same valley is the Corrieshalloch Gorge with the Falls of Measach cascading into this overhung ravine. The site – well worth visiting, if the visitor likes

Below: *Loch Broom is a sea loch stretching many miles inland;* **right:** *the busy fishing port of Ullapool.*
Ci-dessous: *le loch Broom, long loch d'eau de mer;* **à droite:** *Ullapool, petit port de pêche très actif.*
Unten: *Loch Broom ist ein Seeloch, das sich kilometerweit ins Land erstreckt;* **rechts:** *der geschäftige Fischerhafen von Ullapool.*

Left: *the fine sea-scapes of Gruinard Bay;* **above:** *Inverewe Gardens, warmed by the Gulf Stream.*
A gauche: *le beau littoral de Gruinard Bay;* **ci-dessus:** *les jardins d'Inverewe réchauffés par le Gulf Stream.*
Links: *die herrliche Meereslandschaft der Gruinard Bucht;* **oben:** *Inverewe Gärten, die vom Golfstrom erwärmt werden.*

dizzying drops – is managed by the National Trust for Scotland.

The main road back to Inverness runs fast and rolling across the open moors of the Dirrie More with Ben Dearg and its satellites brooding in the north. The equally remote Fannichs – another hill group well off the tourist track – lie southwards. But the empty, speedy stretches of road between Ullapool and Inverness are only one option. At Braemore junction, above the Corrieshalloch Gorge, the A832 doubles back towards Little Loch Broom and the west coast, as if reluctant to cross the backbone of this hard landscape. This section has the name of 'Destitution Road', as a reminder of the 1851 potato famine which happened as the road itself was under construction. Nevertheless, visitors should press on regardless to delightful beaches at Gruinard Bay – and walk along the rocky shore to Stattic Point to admire the wide prospect of An Teallach looming inland.

Further south lies undeniable proof of the warming influence of the Gulf Stream – the unexpected and magnificent Inverewe Gardens, in the care of the National Trust for Scotland. Hudson Bay and Siberia may share the same latitude, but the mild Atlantic airs allow these gardens, founded in the 1870s by Sir Osgood Mackenzie, to boast 2,500 species in their sixty-four acres. What was once a barren peaty headland is now a mass of seasonally-changing colours, with rhododendrons and azaleas particularly conspicuous in late spring.

Gairloch is strung out along its bay, often catching the best of the sun – appreciated by visitors to its uncrowded sandy beach nearby. This small resort has a museum of local life. Hereabouts, too, is a choice of side-roads westwards to explore the little crofting communities on the headlands, or choose a rocky platform on the sea-shore of Loch Ewe to cast a speculative line.

Back on the main road, an eastward swing up Kerrysdale, over the summit moors and down into tall pines, soon brings the visitor to romantic Loch Maree. In spite of its wildness and beauty, the remnant oaks on its shores once saw the encroachment of the first 'modern' iron smelting in Scotland,

Loch Maree
and the Test of True Love

A sad and romantic tale has attached itself to Isle Maree, a wooded island on Ross and Cromarty's most lovely loch. In the ancient days when the Vikings held the north at least partly in their power, a young Viking prince, impetuous and hot-headed in war, but gallant and brave, had fallen in love with a local maiden and wished to marry her. As a leader of a warring band, his military responsibilities clashed with this inconvenient desire for domestic harmony. Much troubled, he consulted the hermit of Isle Maree, a wise old saint, who advised him to build a tower on the island and live at peace with his lady – yet still be within reach of his war-galley, tossing on the salt water of Loch Ewe nearby.

With this ideal solution, he married and spent a blissful winter. But spring soon came, a long-planned warring expedition was at hand and his men urged him to lead them on the raid. He left his sad wife – but not before making a plan to signify their mutual passion. So love-struck were they both, that in order to ease the suspense, they arranged to fly signal flags on his imminent return, as an early indication of each other's well-being. If he were safe, a white flag would flutter from the mast of the

Above and right: *Loch Maree, most beautiful of Highland lochs.*

Ci-dessus et à droite: *le loch Maree, le plus beau loch des Highlands.*

Oben und rechts: *Loch Maree, der schönste der Hochlandseen.*

barge that would ferry him back, while a black flag would signify ill-news. They resolved that the lady would use the same code and, being a two-ferry family, she would sail down the loch on her craft to meet him.

Time passed but luck was with his expedition. His galley tied up once more, he crossed to Loch Maree and, white flag flying, he waited anxiously for a sign as the ferry was rowed down the loch.

But in his absence, some incomprehensible quirk had entered his lady's mind. Perhaps she felt that he did prefer the warring, looting and pillaging life to her company. Tortured by jealousy, she resolved to put this to the test. She prepared a bier on her barge. As his vessel came into view, she hoisted a black flag, climbed aboard and stretched out on the bier, feigning death. The fortuitous presence of her attendants solved the inconvenience of rowing while in this deathly posture and her barge solemnly proceeded up the loch.

As the vessels closed, the prince became frantic with grief. The bows touched and he leapt aboard. In his habitual hot-headed manner he drew his dagger and plunged it into his heart, maddened with grief. At this

spectacular, unforeseen and absolutely fatal demonstration of his true love, the lady leapt from her bier and with a wild shriek of remorse, likewise used the dagger on herself. Mortally wounded, she was carried back to the island where she received last rites from the old saint before dying.

To this day, two ancient graves, a few stones that marked the saint's chapel and a mound said to be the site of the Prince's tower, are to be found on Isle Maree as testimony to the story.

active as early as the first decade of the seventeenth century, using local timber to fire the furnaces. The scars of such activities have long healed, leaving the visitor to enjoy its woodland and the mountain Slioch, 'The Spear', with grey rocky flanks rising steeply from the loch.

The first National Nature Reserve established in the United Kingdom is to be found on the south shore of Loch Maree. The Beinn Eighe reserve has visitor trails (steep in places), to view the ancient pines – relic descendants of the original Caledonian forest – as well as the possibility of pine marten, wildcat, golden eagle and, more likely, red deer.

At Kinlochewe is the gateway to Glen Torridon itself. Westwards along the glen, responsibility for its safekeeping passes from Nature Conservancy Council to National Trust for Scotland. With tempting paths into empty country behind Liathach, or past the bows of this boat-like hill to view the buttresses of Coire Mhic Fhearchair (try 'corry vifferker' and sound like a native), this is walkers' territory.

Left: *Liathach towers over Glen Torridon;* **below:** *Cul Beag and Loch Lurgainn.*
A gauche: *le mont Liathach domine le glen Torridon;* **ci-dessous:** *le mont Cul Beag et le loch Lurgainn.*
Links: *Liathach türmt über Glen Torridon;* **unten:** *Cul Beag und Loch Lurgainn.*

Further east lies Loch Torridon itself with Diabaig reached by a switchback road on its north side which ends abruptly at the local pier after corkscrewing down past crofts and steep fields. On the south side of the loch lies Shieldaig, offering explorations on foot, (go past the church) on to the headland that separates upper and lower Loch Torridon – good for sea-bird spotting, too.

The Applecross peninsula specialises in spectacular sunsets over the hills of Skye, particularly from the Bealach nam Ba. St Maelrubba, who gave his name to Loch Maree, founded a monastery here. Nowadays, with a fairly new road round the north of the peninsula, the spectacular ascent of the Bealach nam Ba – one of the very few Scottish roads that passes through ptarmigan country – can be avoided.

Top left: *sunset over Loch Shieldaig;* **bottom left:** *Loch Torridon;* **above:** *the spectacular Applecross road over Bealach nam Ba.*

A gauche, en haut: *le loch shieldaig;* **en bas:** *le loch Torridon;* **ci-dessus:** *la spectaculaire route d'Applecross.*

Oben links: *Sonnenuntergang über Loch Shieldaig;* **unten links:** *Loch Torridon;* **darüber:** *die einzigartige Applecross Straße über Bealach nam Ba.*

Down in this southern corner of Ross and Cromarty, where the deep waters of Loch Kishorn have proved attractive to oil-platform builders, Lochcarron is the local centre, a pretty village with a wide range of shops, along the waterfront. Between Lochcarron and Shieldaig is the tiny, and often overlooked, Rassal ash wood, a fenced-in Nature Reserve to be viewed from the outside. Worth stopping a few minutes here, for an interesting lesson in how the landscape of the Highlands has been changed. By keeping out sheep and deer, an unexpected lushness of vegetation has developed with a wide range of flora, as well as the most northerly occurrence of the ash tree in the UK. Comparing this to the well-cropped pasture and the acid moorlands which surround the reserve, the visitor is reminded that even in 'wilderness Scotland', centuries of land use by man – cutting, burning, grazing – has affected this landscape too – just as surely as it formed the neat fields and trimmed hedges of the contrasting south.

Left: *Plockton, famous for its colourful gardens;* **below:** *the ash occurs in lime-rich outcrops in the Highlands.*
A gauche: *Plockton, célèbre pour ses jardins;* **ci-dessous:** *le frêne pousse sur les affleurements calcaires.*
Links: *Plockton ist berühmt für seine bunten Gärten;* **unten:** *die Esche gedeiht auf kalkreichem Boden im Hochland.*

Wildlife

The remoteness of parts of Ross and Cromarty make it an ideal and undisturbed habitat for a wide range of wildlife. The largest is the red deer (*bottom left*), found in considerable numbers in the west and central parts. Females, after calving, retreat to secure hill slopes to tend their young undisturbed. The same need for seclusion is felt by the golden eagle (*top left*), which usually chooses a rocky ledge for its nest site. Casual observers should not confuse it with the buzzard, often found at lower altitudes and of a smaller build and generally lighter coloration. Another bird that can be hard to identify at extreme range is the black-throated diver (*centre left*); handsome in its breeding plumage, it prefers remote moorland lochs of a greater size than does its near cousin the red-throated diver. Among the invertebrates, the open grasslands are the habitat of the Scotch Argus (*below*). Less intensive farming methods and less use of pesticides in the west mean that there is a surprising range of butterflies to be observed.

A gauche en haut; *aigle royal;* **au centre:** *plongeon;* **en bas:** *cerf;* **ci-dessous:** *papillon Scotch Argus.*

Oben links: *Steinadler;* **Mitte links:** *Prachttaucher;* **unten links:** *Rotwild;* **unten:** *Scotch Argus Schmetterling.*

The Brahan Seer

The best known of the Highland seers – exponents of the 'second sight' – was Coinneach Odhar (pronounced 'co-in-yach oar') or Brown Kenneth, the Brahan Seer, who lived in the first half of the seventeenth century. He remains mysterious in these modern times, after centuries and profound cultural changes have obscured the original Gaelic culture. Oral tradition has also added to his exploits and the legends as we know them today perhaps incorporate other predictions by other Gaels with this strange gift.

Among his many utterances, he is credited with predicting the construction of the Caledonian Canal, improved road communications, depopulation through sheep farming, the Battle of Culloden, the coming of the railways and even, it is firmly believed by the people of Inverness, the Second World War. In addition there is a wealth of prophecy of lesser significance, as well as those connected with the Seaforth family.

In this body of documented writings, there are unfulfilled predictions, too, among which there is the chilling '. . . the people will emigrate to Islands now unknown . . . after which the deer and other wild animals in the huge wilderness will be exterminated and browned by horrid black rains. The people will then return and take undisturbed possession of the lands of their ancestors.' This often-quoted and much-feared prophecy, which starts with reference to the Highland clearances, ends with an allusion to some ghastly event. Some have decided it is connected with developments in the oil industry taking place locally. Others, most disturbingly of all, think in terms of nuclear fall-out.

The commemorative stone placed at Chanonry Point in 1969 marks the spot, traditionally, where the seer met his end. He was burned in a spiked tar-barrel after a spectacularly unappreciated party-trick. Lady Seaforth had invited him to amuse some guests whom she was entertaining while her husband was on the Continent. On being asked if he could see what her husband was doing in Paris at that precise moment, he had the tactlessness to be absolutely truthful. At this affront, the Countess ordered his demise. Interestingly, this traditional tale of his horrible end, just before which he predicted the downfall of the family, echoes the trial for witchcraft of a similarly named warlock a century earlier. Some say that the seer did not die in this manner, but lived to a ripe old age.

Whatever the truth of the matter, there are many people today who still believe that the wealth of local detail contained in the prophecies gives an authentic ring to many . . . and that some will yet be fulfilled.

Top: *the Caledonian Canal, mentioned in the prophecies of the Brahan Seer, who cruelly met his death at Chanonry Point* **(above)**.

En haut: *le Canal Calédonien, prédit par le prophète de Brahan, qui connut une mort violente à Chanonry Point* **(ci-dessus)**.

Oben: *der kaledonische Kanal, der in den Prophezeiungen des Brahan Seher erwähnt wird. Letzterer erlitt am Chanonry Point einen grausamen Tod* **(darunter)**.

Activities for visitors

Check with your local tourist information centre for the local Highland games. These events, which were once trials held by the local clan chief to find not only the best warriors or bodyguards but also the best musicians and dancers, are held throughout Scotland during the summer months. Another event with traditional roots is the ceilidh, once a gathering of story tellers and singers within a house, as part of the community's social activities. Now this function is mainly taken over by hotels, but the entertainment still takes place with varying degrees of tradition.

Traditional ways of life are on display at museums at Ullapool, Dingwall, Tain and Gairloch. Cruising to the Summer Isles from Ullapool will reveal aspects of a traditional sea-going life now vanished. The old fish-curing station and ruined pier on Tanera, the largest of the Summer Isles, are evidence of a once-thriving industry in this remote part of Wester Ross. There is also a ferry to the island from Achiltibuie opposite.

This little village, with its sandy beach, is only one of a number of bases for sea-angling. Aultbea, Ullapool, Gairloch, Badachro and Portmahomack also have craft for hire. For visitors seeking the delights of sandy beaches, Gruinard Bay, Opinan, Red Point, Cromarty, Fortrose and Rosemarkie are only a few of the stretches on

Left: *Highland dancing features at Highland Games;* **below:** *walking is a popular pastime.*
A gauche: *danse typique des Highlands;* **ci-dessous:** *populaires randonnées.*
Links: *Hochlandtänze bei den Hochlandspielen;* **unten:** *Wandern ist eine beliebte Freizeiterholung.*